First Picture Dictionary
Animals
قَامُوسُ الصُّوَرِ الأَوَّلُ
الحَيَوَانَاتُ

Pig
خِنزِيرٌ

Rabbit
أَرنَبٌ

Butterfly
فَرَاشَةٌ

Fox
ثَعلَبٌ

Illustrated by Anna Ivanir

www.kidkiddos.com
Copyright ©2025 by KidKiddos Books Ltd.
support@kidkiddos.com

All rights reserved. No part of this book may be reproduced in any form or by any electronic or mechanical means, including information storage and retrieval systems, without written permission from the publisher, except in the case of a reviewer, who may quote brief passages embodied in critical articles or in a review.
First edition, 2025

Library and Archives Canada Cataloguing in Publication
First Picture Dictionary - Animals (English Arabic Bilingual edition)
ISBN: 978-1-83416-267-6 paperback
ISBN: 978-1-83416-268-3 hardcover
ISBN: 978-1-83416-266-9 eBook

Wild Animals
الحَيَواناتُ البَرِّيَّةُ

Lion
أسَدٌ

Tiger
نَمِرٌ

Giraffe
زَرافَةٌ

✦ *A giraffe is the tallest animal on land.*
✦الزَّرافَةُ هِيَ أطوَلُ حَيَوانٍ عَلَى اليابِسَةِ.

Elephant
فِيلٌ

Monkey
قِردٌ

Wild Animals
الحَيَواناتُ البَرِّيَّةُ

Hippopotamus
فَرسُ النَّهرِ

Panda
باندا

Fox
ثَعَلَبٌ

Rhino
وَحِيدُ القَرنِ

Deer
غَزالٌ

Moose
أَيِّل

Wolf
ذِئْبٌ

Squirrel
سِنْجابٌ

✦ A moose is a great swimmer and can dive underwater to eat plants!

✦ الأَيِّلُ سَبَّاحٌ ماهِرٌ ويَغوصُ تَحتَ الماءِ لِيَأْكُلَ النَّباتاتِ!

Koala
كُوالا

✦ A squirrel hides nuts for winter, but sometimes forgets where it put them!

✦ يُخَبِّئُ السِّنْجابُ الجَوزَ لِلشِّتاءِ، وَلَكِنَّهُ أحيانًا يَنسى أينَ وَضَعَهُ!

Gorilla
غُوريلّا

Pets
الحَيَواناتُ الأَلِيفَةُ

Canary
كَناريٌّ

Guinea Pig
خنزير غينيا

✦ A frog can breathe through its skin as well as its lungs!
✦ يَستَطيعُ الضِّفدَعُ أَن يَتَنَفَّسَ مِن جِلدِهِ وَرِئَتَيهِ!

Frog
ضِفدَعٌ

Hamster
هامِستَر

Goldfish
سَمَكَةٌ ذَهَبِيَّةٌ

Dog
كَلبٌ

> ✦ *Some parrots can copy words and even laugh like a human!*
> ✦ بَعضُ البَبَّغاواتِ يُمكِنُها تَقليدُ الكَلِماتِ وَالضَّحِكُ مِثلَ الإنسانِ!

Parrot
بَبَّغاءٌ

Cat
قِطٌّ

Animals at the Farm
حَيواناتُ المَزرعَةِ

Cow
بَقَرَةٌ

Chicken
دَجاجَةٌ

Duck
بَطَّةٌ

Sheep
خَروفٌ

Horse
حِصانٌ

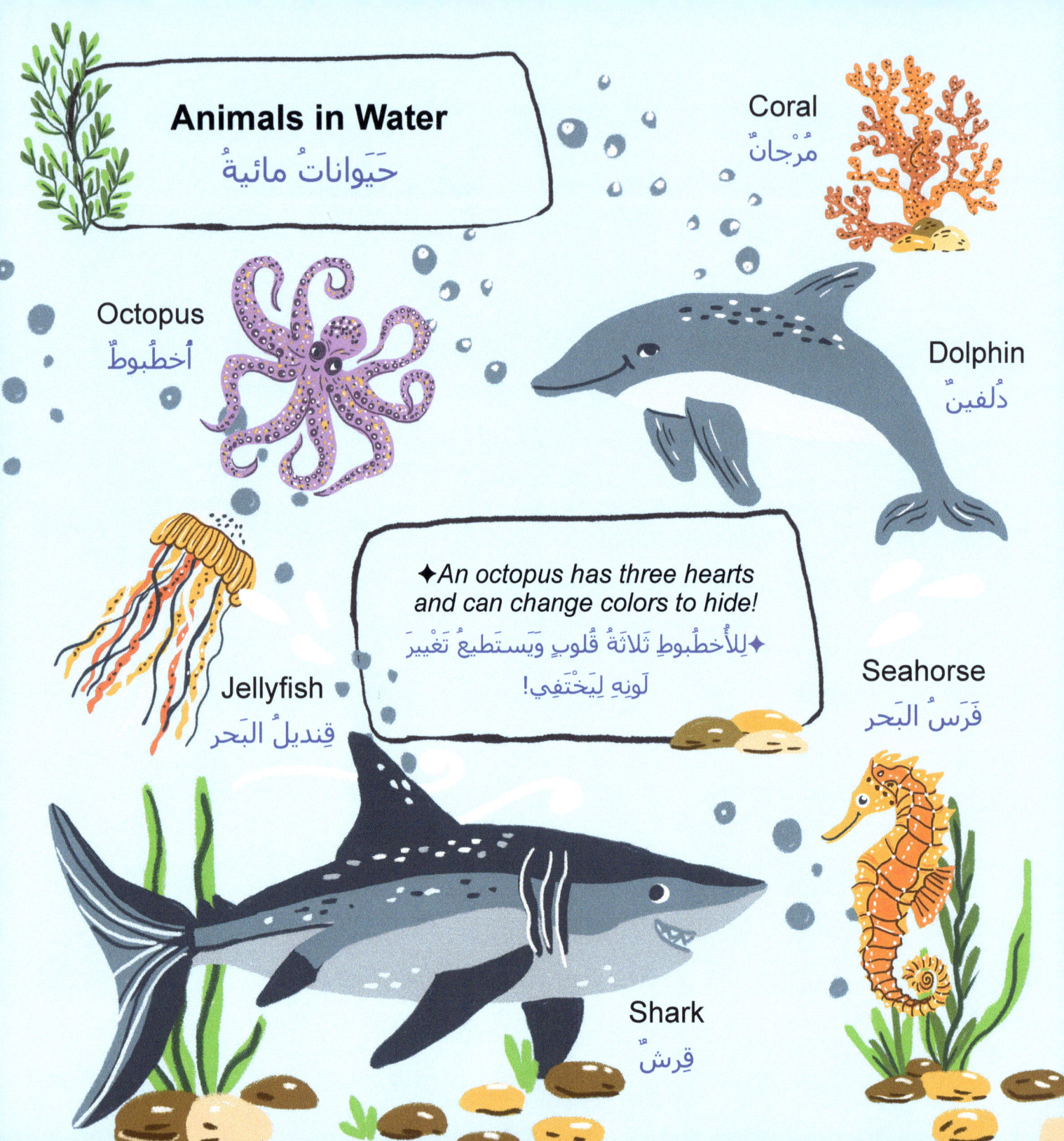

Small Animals
حَيَوَانَات صَغِيرَة

Chameleon
حَرْبَاء

Spider
عَنْكَبُوت

✦ *An ostrich is the biggest bird, but it cannot fly!*

✦ النَّعَامَة أَكْبَر طَائِر، وَلَكِنَّهَا لَا تَسْتَطِيع الطَّيَرَان!

Bee
نَحْلَة

✦ *A snail carries its home on its back and moves very slowly.*

✦ يَحْمِل الحَلَزُون بَيْتَهُ عَلَى ظَهْرِه وَيَتَحَرَّك بِبُطْء شَدِيد.

Snail
حَلَزُون

Mouse
فَأْر

Quiet Animals
الحَيَواناتُ الهادِئَةُ

Turtle
سُلْحْفَاةٌ

Ladybug
خُنْفَسَاءٌ مُنَقَّطَةٌ

✦ A turtle can live both on land and in water.
✦ يُمْكِنُ لِلسُّلْحْفَاةِ أَنْ تَعِيشَ فِي الْبَرِّ وَفِي الْمَاءِ.

Fish
سَمَكَةٌ

Lizard
سِحْلِيَّةٌ

Owl
بُومَةٌ

Bat
خُفَّاشٌ

✦An owl hunts at night and uses its hearing to find food!
✦تَصْطَادُ الْبُومَةُ لَيْلًا وَتَسْتَخْدِمُ سَمْعَهَا لِتَجِدَ الطَّعَامَ!

✦A firefly glows at night to find other fireflies.
✦تَتَوَهَّجُ الْيَرَقَانَةُ لِتَجِدَ آخَرِينَ مِنْ نَوْعِهَا.

Raccoon
رَاكُونٌ

Tarantula
عِنْكَبُوتُ تَرِنْتُولَا

Colorful Animals
اَلْحَيَوَانَاتُ الْمُلَوَّنَةُ

A flamingo is pink
الْفْلَامِنْغُو لَوْنُهُ وَرْدِيٌّ

An owl is brown
الْبُومَةُ لَوْنُهَا بُنِّيٌّ

A swan is white
الْبَجَعَةُ لَوْنُهَا أَبْيَضُ

An octopus is purple
الْأُخْطُبُوطُ لَوْنُهُ أُرْجُوَانِيٌّ

A frog is green
الضفدع لونهُ أخضر

✦ A frog is green, so it can hide among the leaves.
✦ الضَّفْدَع أخْضَرُ اللَّوْنِ لِيَستَطَيع الِاخْتِبَاءَ بَيْنَ الْأَوْرَاقِ.

Animals and Their Babies
اَلْحَيَوَانَاتُ وَصِغَارُهَا

Cow and Calf
بَقَرَةٌ وَعِجْلٌ

Cat and Kitten
قِطَّةٌ وهِرَّة

✦ *A chick talks to its mother even before it hatches.*
✦ الكَتْكُوت يُخَاطِبُ أُمَّهُ حَتَّى قَبْلَ أَنْ يَفْقِسَ.

Chicken and Chick
الدجاجة والكتكوت

Dog and Puppy
كَلْبٌ وَجَرْوٌ

Butterfly and Caterpillar
فَرَاشَةٌ وَيَرْقَانَةٌ

Sheep and Lamb
خَرُوفٌ وَحَمَلٌ

Horse and Foal
حِصَانٌ وَمُهْرٌ

Pig and Piglet
خِنْزِيرٌ وَخِنْزِيرٌ صَغِيرٌ

Goat and Kid
مَاعِزٌ وَجَدْيٌ

www.ingramcontent.com/pod-product-compliance
Lightning Source LLC
LaVergne TN
LVHW072055060526
838200LV00061B/4743